MW01234837

# THE ULTIMATE

# NINJA® Foodi

# COOKBOOK 2021

**The most comprehensive guide
to mastering your Multicooker.**

*Steaming, air frying, grilling and searing your favorite meals in no time!*

© Copyright 2021 - Cookbook Academy by Ciro Russo

All rights reserved.

The content contained within this book may not be reproduced, duplicated or transmitted without direct written permission from the author or the publisher. Under no circumstances will any blame or legal responsibility be held against the publisher, or author, for any damages, reparation, or monetary loss due to the information contained within this book. Either directly or indirectly.

Legal Notice: This book is copyright protected. This book is only for personal use. You cannot amend, distribute, sell, use, quote or paraphrase any part, or the content within this book, without the consent of the author or publisher.

Disclaimer Notice: Please note the information contained within this document is for educational and entertainment purposes only. All effort has been executed to present accurate, up to date, and reliable, complete information. No warranties of any kind are declared or implied. Readers acknowledge that the author is not engaging in the rendering of legal, financial, medical or professional advice. The content within this book has been derived from various sources. Please consult a licensed professional before attempting any techniques outlined in this book.

By reading this document, the reader agrees that under no circumstances is the author responsible for any losses, direct or indirect, which are incurred as a result of the use of information contained within this document, including, but not limited to, — errors, omissions, or inaccuracies.

Book writing: Cookbook Academy Staff

Interior and Cover Designer: Laura Antonioli
Editor: Matt Smith
Production Manager: LP Business & Management LTD
Production Editor: Ash Rowling
Photography © 2020/2021: Janet Specter

COOKBOOK ACADEMY 2021 - by Ciro Russo

Given the great success of our publications, here are the links to other books written by us:

The Ultimate Emeril Lagasse Power Air Fryer 360 Plus Cookbook 202:
https://www.amazon.com/dp/B093RV4VMY

Pilot Kitchen - https://www.amazon.com/dp/B08TY8D66N

# Table of Contents

## Pork, Beef and Lamb • 53

## Conclusions • 67

Introduction

## What is the ninja foodi?

*If you already have this versatile multicooker you know the answer, but if you don't have it yet or if you are not sure about its usefulness and want to know more about its performance... go here!*

*The ninja foodi is an innovative multifunctional cooker that can be used as a slow cooker, steamer, fryer, pan, roaster, broiler, dehydrator...*

*Great, isn't it? with just one kitchen tool you can prepare stews, meats, snacks, desserts and dehydrate fruits and vegetables so they keep for a long time!*

*With the invaluable help of this guide you can master your foodi and know every secret, prepare countless recipes for your family and get the results you love, especially with the help of the "tender-crisp" technology that characterizes this tool and makes it irreplaceable: tender and succulent dishes with a deliciously crisp finish, a delight for the palate and eyes. ...*

*Using the ninja foodi air fryer you can cook with ease, in a short time and without dirtying your kitchen, obtaining optimal results both in terms of taste and health of your loved ones. you will also save a lot of money...*

*Have you ever been hungry and tired of cooking at home, so you decided to order take-out or go to a restaurant?*

*It's a bit of a waste, don't you think? it's also not very healthy because of the amount and quality of fats it contains... But you don't have to worry anymore because now you can make your ninja food: the best recipe you can use!*

## Do you feel like trying?

*Then what are you waiting for, unleash the chef in you!!!*

### Ratings

In all of our cookbooks you'll find a grade of evaluation on each individual recipe called "Ratings".

The "Ratings" goes from 1 to 5 stars and it is determined by the complexity of the dish and the time you'll need to prepare it.

1 star will indicate a very quick and easy meal, while 5 stars will be a more complex recipe with higher preparation time needed.

We wanted to offer you this method of evaluating on every dish in order to make it even easier for you to choose the most suitable recipes according to your time availability.

**Cookbook Academy Team**

The Ninja Foodi
Digital Air Fry
Oven Basics

The Ninja Foodi Air Fry is the ultimate meal-making machine. It is a convection oven with smart-programmed features that lets you cook a complete dish meal using just one kitchen device.

**Functionalities:**

- **Air Fry:** It allows air frying without or less oil added.

- **Air Roast:** It produces perfectly browned, crispy, and evenly-cooked dishes, like a full-sized sheet pan with roasted vegetables.

- **Air Broil:** It allows you to broil fish and meat and brown casserole tops evenly.

- **Bake:** It allows you to conveniently bake pastries, desserts, and snacks.

- **Dehydrate:** It is useful for dehydrating meat, vegetables, and fruits.

- **Keep Warm:** It can keep your food warm up to 2 hours.

- **Toast:** It allows you to toast up to 9 bread slices simultaneously with "Light," "Dark," and "Brown" options.

- **Bagel:** You can perfectly toast up to 9 bagel halves when placed cut-side up on the wire rack.

## Advantages of Using Ninja Digital Air Fry Oven

Made of High-Quality Material

The oven is made of stainless steel with rounded edges and coated with a superb finishing that makes it look elegant and classy. This material gives the air fryer durability and strength. With careful use, the oven could last for years.

Save Enough Counter Space

The Air Fry Oven takes up 50% less space in your countertop or cabinet, as you can have the option to flip it up and store it. It has an adjustable flip function that allows you to keep the oven in both vertical and horizontal positions on your counter or kitchen shelf—depending on available space. However, when you are ready to store it while not in use, simply flip it up and it can stand in a vertical position, leaving more space (about 50%) on your shelf for your other kitchen appliance.

Another thing that makes this Air Fry Oven a real space saver is the fact that you won't need toasters, as the Ninja Foodie Digital Air Fry Oven is also a useful toaster that gives you two options for toasting bread slices and bagel. Simply press the "Toast" button for bread or the "Bagel" button for toasting a bagel.

You can adjust the temperature and time for toasts when you press the "Darkness" button and "Slices" button. These functions can provide you with a crispy dark brown or soft light brown toast depending on what you desire.

Speed Cooking

It can Cook 60% faster compared to when you're using a traditional oven with an air roast. You can preheat the oven in 60 seconds and have a full meal in as little as 20 minutes.

Ninja Digital
Air Fry Oven
Smart Settings

It is very easy to follow as each button in the control signifies every function.

Functions and modes are right below the LED panel. It has a multifunctional dial that serves as the selector for the preferred function and also starts/pauses the oven. The "Temperature" and "Time" buttons are for adjusting the cooking temperature and time. There is also an adjustment for the darkness level and the number of slices for the "Toast" mode. The current mode is indicated by the blue light.

The "ON" and "OFF" power buttons can be found close to the control panel.

Air Fry:

- Heat Source/Airflow: High heat from top and bottom
- Desired Result or Effect: Quick and extra-crispy effect with little or no oil
- Requirement: An air fryer with or without sheet pan
- Best for: French fries (freshly cut or frozen), chicken wings, and vegetables

Air Roast:

- Heat Source/Airflow: Even heat from top and bottom
- Desired Result or Effect: A dish that is crispy on the outside but juicy inside

- Requirement: A sheet pan
- Best for: Sheet pan meals, whole meat, and vegetables

Air Broil:

- Heat Source/Airflow: High heat from top
- Desired Result or Effect: Top-down heat for a crispy effect
- Best for: Fish, nachos, steak, and for finishing casseroles
- Requirement: A sheet pan

Bake:

- Heat Source/Airflow: High, even heat from top and bottom
- Desired Result or Effect: Overall even cooking with a light-browning effect
- Best for: Cookies, cakes, and frozen pizza
- Requirement: Use a sheet pan

Toast:

- Heat Source/Airflow: Even heat from top and bottom
- Desired Result or Effect: Quick even browning effect on both sides
- Best for: English muffins, bread, and frozen waffles
- Requirement: Use a wire rack

Bagel:

- Heat Source/Airflow: Slightly lower heat from the top than the bottom
- Desired Result or Effect: Quick, even browning
- Best for: Bagels and artisan bread
- Requirement: A wire rack

Dehydrate:

- Heat Source/Airflow: Low Heat
- Desired Result or Effect: Removed moisture for jerky and dried fruits
- Best for: Jerky and dried fruits
- Requirement: The air fryer basket with or without sheet pan

Dehydrating

When you want to make use of the dehydration feature of the Ninja Foodi Digital Air Fry, here are some kitchen tips to make things easier and better.

To lessen dehydrating time and save on energy, you need to slice fruits and vegetables to a thin size. It would be easier to use a mandolin slicer to produce uniformed cuts.

Some fruits oxidize when cut. Soak them in water mixed with squeezed lemon extract for 5 minutes. This will prevent discoloration and help them retain their color while undergoing the process of dehydration.

Before adding fruits and veggies to your Air Fry Oven to dehydrate, pat them dry with paper towels.

Lay each piece of the food flat on the air fry basket without stacking them or overlapping them with each other so that the circulating hot air can easily reach them.

On average, fruits and vegetables require low heat (135°F) and takes about 6–8 hours to dehydrate. When dehydrating fresh food, check every 6 hours to monitor the degree of doneness and prevent the food from getting burnt.

You can maximize the longevity of dehydrated food by storing them at room temperature in an air-tight container for up to two weeks. If you plan to dehydrate fish and meat, it is recommended that you roast them at 330°F for about 1 minute as a final step to completely pasteurize them. For jerky, it gets crispier when you dehydrate them longer.

# Taking Care of Your Air Fryer

Regular cleaning is essential to ensure that your Ninja Foodi Digital Air Fry Oven can last long, regular cleaning is essential. We have here two guides to cleaning your revolutionary kitchen device.

For Everyday Cleaning

After each use, unplug your Ninja Foodi Digital Air Fry Oven from the wall outlet. But before cleaning, make sure that it has cooled off as the oven can be very hot and can burn your skin. You will see the "HOT" sign in red that will tell you that the cooling is still in progress. Once it has completely cooled down, the "HOT" sign will disappear, which means that it is now ready for cleaning and you can now unplug the oven to cut the power supply. You can then start taking out all the removable parts including the wire rack, sheet pan, air fryer basket, and crumb tray.

For Deep Cleaning

Make sure that you have unplugged your Ninja Foodi Digital Air Fry Oven from the wall outlet or socket and have left it to cool down.

Start removing all accessories from your Air Fry Oven, including the crumb tray. Wash each accessory separately. Note that all parts of the Ninja Foodi Digital Air Fry Oven are dishwasher-friendly.

Flip the oven up into the storage position and press the "Push" button to release the back door. This will provide you access to the interior of the Air Fry Oven.

To flip the air fryer up, hold the handle under the lid and try pushing its front upward. Then pull the base of the oven and it will likewise come out like the lid. Also, wipe the base with a damp cloth and allow complete drying for the base before closing it.

# Digital Time and Temperature Setting

To set cooking time, simply press the "Time" button and rotate the dial to the desired time. To set the cooking temperature, set the "Temp" button and rotate the dial to set it to the desired temperature. To start cooking, press on the dial.

When setting, the temperature range can vary depending on the function.

- For air frying, the temperature range can be between 250–450°F.

- For air roasting, the temperature range can be between 250–450°F.

- For air broiling, the temperature range can be between 350–450°F (high).

- For baking, the temperature range can be between 250–400°F.

- For toasting, the temperature can be up to 450°F.

- For dehydrating, the temperature range can be between 105–195°F.

- For warming food previously cooked, the temperature can be up to 165°F.

When setting the cooking time, the time increments can vary also depending on the preferred function.

- For air frying, the time increment is 1 min–1 hour.

- For air roasting, the time increment is 1 min–2 hours.

- For air broiling, the time increment is 30 sec–30 min.

- For air baking, the time increment is 1 min–2 hours.

- For toasting, the time increment is 30 sec–10 min, depending on the "Darkness" and "Slice" settings.

- For dehydrating, the time increment is 30 min–12 hours.

- For keeping food warm, the time increment is 5 min–2 hours.

Features of Ninja Foodi Digital Air Fry Oven

## Air Fry Basket

The flat air fry basket accommodates more food compared to the rounded one currently available in most air fryer models. You can evenly spread your food out to produce an even distribution of hot air, resulting in well-browned crisp air fried dishes.

Depending on your recipe, the basket can hold up to 4 lb. of food, but to ensure even cooking, follow the directions in your recipe. It is also non-stick, so it is not necessary to spray it with cooking oil to prevent it from sticking.

## Sheet Pan

The Ninja Foodi Digital Air Fry Oven comes with a sheet pan that sits just below the air fry basket, catching any falling crumbs or dripping grease from the food you are cooking. There is neither grove nor space to allow the pan to be moved without moving the air fryer basket, and vice versa. So when removing the hot air fryer basket while cooking, you need to keep in mind removing it together with the pan to avoid accidentally having it landed on your foot.

## Side Blower

The Ninja Foodi Digital Air Fry Oven blows in the air coming from the sides as opposed to the usual top-down approach use by most air fryers. When the food is evenly spread on the air fryer basket, the hot air coming in from the sides can produce a crispier result and a more even browning.

## The Control Panel

You would not find it difficult to navigate through your cooking experiences as the digital control panel on the Ninja Foodie Digital Air Fry Oven is easy to read and understand. The interface is fairly intuitive to set and is centered on a knob or dial that you can turn to set the cooking time and temperature for each function. It also allows you to select the number of slices and doneness.

The Ninja Foodie Digital Air Fry Oven has a LED screen just above the control panel that displays the temperature in "F" as well as the cooking time in minutes and hours. If the oven is preheating, you will see "Pre" displayed on the screen, or "Hot" if it needs a little cooling. Once it has cooled enough, the display will show "Flip," which means that the Air Fry Oven can now be flipped and ready to be stored.

# COOKING CONVERSION CHART

## Measurement

| CUP | ONCES | MILLILITERS | TABLESPOONS |
|---|---|---|---|
| 8 cup | 64 oz | 1895 ml | 128 |
| 6 cup | 48 oz | 1420 ml | 96 |
| 5 cup | 40 oz | 1180 ml | 80 |
| 4 cup | 32 oz | 960 ml | 64 |
| 2 cup | 16 oz | 480 ml | 32 |
| 1 cup | 8 oz | 240 ml | 16 |
| 3/4 cup | 6 oz | 177 ml | 12 |
| 2/3 cup | 5 oz | 158 ml | 11 |
| 1/2 cup | 4 oz | 118 ml | 8 |
| 3/8 cup | 3 oz | 90 ml | 6 |
| 1/3 cup | 2.5 oz | 79 ml | 5.5 |
| 1/4 cup | 2 oz | 59 ml | 4 |
| 1/8 cup | 1 oz | 30 ml | 3 |
| 1/16 cup | 1/2 oz | 15 ml | 1 |

## Temperature

| FAHRENHEIT | CELSIUS |
|---|---|
| 100 °F | 37 °C |
| 150 °F | 65 °C |
| 200 °F | 93 °C |
| 250 °F | 121 °C |
| 300 °F | 150 °C |
| 325 °F | 160 °C |
| 350 °F | 180 °C |
| 375 °F | 190 °C |
| 400 °F | 200 °C |
| 425 °F | 220 °C |
| 450 °F | 230 °C |
| 500 °F | 260 °C |
| 525 °F | 274 °C |
| 550 °F | 288 °C |

## Weight

| IMPERIAL | METRIC |
|---|---|
| 1/2 oz | 15 g |
| 1 oz | 29 g |
| 2 oz | 57 g |
| 3 oz | 85 g |
| 4 oz | 113 g |
| 5 oz | 141 g |
| 6 oz | 170 g |
| 8 oz | 227 g |
| 10 oz | 283 g |
| 12 oz | 340 g |
| 13 oz | 369 g |
| 14 oz | 397 g |
| 15 oz | 425 g |
| 1 lb | 453 g |

Poultry

# Cajun Spiced Whole Chicken

 Preparation time
15 MINUTES

 Cooking time
1 HOUR 10 MINUTES

Servings
6

## Ratings

## Ingredients

¼ cup butter, softened
2 tsp. dried rosemary
2 tsp. dried thyme
1 tbsp. Cajun seasoning
1 tbsp. onion powder
1 tbsp. garlic powder
1 tbsp. paprika
1 tsp. cayenne pepper
Salt, as required
1 (3-lb.) whole chicken, neck and giblets removed

## Nutritional Info

Calories: 421
Fats: 14.8 g
Saturated Fats: 6.9 g
Carbs: 2.3 g
Fiber: 0.9 g
Sugar: 0.5 g
Protein: 66.3 g

## Directions

1. In a bowl, add the butter, herbs, spices and salt and mix well.
2. Rub the chicken with spicy mixture generously.
3. With the help of kitchen twines, tie off the wings and legs.
4. Press the "Power" button of the Ninja Foodi Digital Air Fry Oven and turn the dial to select "Air Bake" mode.
5. Press the "Time" button and again turn the dial to set the cooking time to 70 minutes.
6. Now push the "Temp" button and rotate the dial to set the temperature at 380°F.
7. Press the "Start/Pause" button to start.
8. Open the unit when it has reached the temperature, when it beeps.
9. Arrange the chicken over the wire rack and insert them in the Air Fry Oven.
10. When the cooking time is completed, open the lid and place the chicken onto a platter for about 10 minutes before cutting.
11. Cut into desired sized pieces and serve.

# Lemony Whole Chicken

| | | |
|---|---|---|
| **Preparation time** | **Cooking time** | **Servings** |
| 15 MINUTES | 1 HOUR 20 MINUTES | 8 |

## Ratings

## Ingredients

1 (5-lb.) whole chicken, neck and giblets removed

Salt and ground black pepper, as required

2 fresh rosemary sprigs

1 small onion, peeled and quartered

1 garlic clove

4 lemon zest slices

1 tbsp. extra-virgin olive oil

1 tbsp. fresh lemon juice

## Nutritional Info

Calories: 448

Fats: 10.4 g

Saturated Fats: 2.7 g

Carbs: 1 g

Fiber: 0.4 g

Sugar: 0.2 g

Protein: 82 g

## Directions

1. Rub the chicken with salt and black pepper evenly.
2. Place the rosemary sprigs, onion quarters, garlic halves and lemon zest in the cavity of the chicken.
3. With the help of kitchen twines, tie off the wings and legs.
4. Arrange the chicken onto a greased baking pan and drizzle with the oil and lemon juice.
5. Press the "Power" button of the Ninja Foodi Digital Air Fry Oven and turn the dial to select "Air Bake" mode.
6. Press the "Time" button and again turn the dial to set the cooking time to 20 minutes.
7. Now push the "Temp" button and rotate the dial to set the temperature at 400°F.
8. Press the "Start/Pause" button to start.
9. Open the unit when it has reached the temperature, when it beeps.
10. Arrange the pan over the wire rack and insert them in the oven.
11. After 20 minutes of cooking, set the temperature to 375°F for 60 minutes.
12. When cooking time is completed, open the lid and place the chicken onto a platter for about 10 minutes before cutting.
13. Cut into desired piece sizes and serve.

Serving Suggestions: Serve alongside the steamed veggies.

Variation Tip: Lemon can be replaced with lime.

# Crispy Chicken Legs

**Preparation time**
15 MINUTES

**Cooking time**
20 MINUTES

**Servings**
3

## Ratings

## Ingredients

3 (8-oz.) chicken legs
1 cup buttermilk
2 cups white flour
1 tsp. garlic powder
1 tsp. onion powder
1 tsp. ground cumin
1 tsp. paprika
Salt and ground black pepper, as required
1 tbsp. olive oil

## Nutritional Info

Calories: 817
Fats: 23.3 g
Saturated Fats: 5.9 g
Carbs: 69.5 g
Fiber: 2.7 g
Sugar: 4.7 g
Protein: 77.4 g

## Directions

1. In a bowl, place the chicken legs and buttermilk and refrigerate for about 2 hours.
2. In a shallow dish, mix together the flour and the spices.
3. Remove the chicken from buttermilk.
4. Coat the chicken legs with flour mixture, then dip them into buttermilk and finally, coat with the flour mixture again.
5. Press the "Power" of the Ninja Foodi Digital Air Fry Oven and turn the dial to select "Air Fry" mode.
6. Press the "Time" button and again turn the dial to set the cooking time to 20 minutes.
7. Now push the "Temp" button and rotate the dial to set the temperature to 355°F.
8. Press the "Start/Pause" button to start.
9. When the unit beeps to show that it is preheated, open the lid and grease the air fry basket.
10. Arrange the chicken legs into the prepared air fry basket and drizzle with the oil.
11. Insert the basket in the Air Fry Oven.
12. When cooking time is completed, open the lid and serve hot.

Serving Suggestions: Serve with your favorite dip.
Variation Tip: White flour can be replaced with almond flour too.

# Marinated Spicy Chicken Legs

 **Preparation time**
10 MINUTES

 **Cooking time**
20 MINUTES

 **Servings**
4

## Ratings

## Ingredients

4 chicken legs
3 tbsp. fresh lemon juice
3 tsp. ginger paste
3 tsp. garlic paste
Salt, as required
4 tbsp. plain yogurt
2 tsp. red chili powder
1 tsp. ground cumin
1 tsp. ground coriander
1 tsp. ground turmeric
Ground black pepper, as required

## Nutritional Info

Calories: 461
Fats: 17.6 g
Saturated Fats: 5 g
Carbs: 4.3 g
Fiber: 0.9 g
Sugar: 1.5 g
Protein: 67.1 g

## Directions

1. In a bowl, mix together the chicken legs, lemon juice, ginger, garlic and salt. Set aside for about 15 minutes.
2. Meanwhile, in another bowl, mix together the yogurt and the spices.
3. Add the chicken legs and coat with the spice mixture generously.
4. Cover the bowl and refrigerate for at least 10–12 hours.
5. Press the "Power" button of the Ninja Foodi Digital Air Fry Oven and turn the dial to select "Air Fry" mode.
6. Press the "Time" button and again turn the dial to set the cooking time to 20 minutes.
7. Now push the "Temp" button and rotate the dial to set the temperature to 440°F.
8. Press the "Start/Pause" button to start.
9. When the unit beeps to show that it is preheated, open the lid and grease the air fry basket.
10. Place the chicken legs into the prepared air fry basket and insert them in the Air Fry Oven.
11. When cooking time is completed, open the lid and serve hot.

Serving Suggestions: Serve with fresh greens.

Variation Tip: Lemon juice can be replaced with vinegar.

# Crispy Chicken Drumsticks

 **Preparation time**
15 MINUTES

 **Cooking time**
25 MINUTES

**Servings**
4

## Ratings

## Ingredients

4 chicken drumsticks

1 tbsp. adobo seasoning

Salt, as required

1 tbsp. onion powder

1 tbsp. garlic powder

½ tbsp. paprika

Ground black pepper, as required

2 eggs

2 tbsp. milk

1 cup all-purpose flour

¼ cup cornstarch

## Nutritional Info

Calories: 483

Fats: 12.5 g

Saturated Fats: 3.4 g

Carbs: 35.1 g

Fiber: 1.6 g

Sugar: 1.8 g

Protein: 53.7 g

## Directions

1. Season the chicken drumsticks with the adobo seasoning and a pinch of salt.
2. Set aside for about 5 minutes.
3. In a small bowl, add the spices, salt and black pepper and mix well.
4. In a shallow bowl, add the eggs, milk and 1 tsp. of the spice mixture and beat until well combined.
5. In another shallow bowl, add the flour, cornstarch and the remaining spice mixture.
6. Coat the chicken drumsticks with the flour mixture and tap off excess.
7. Now, dip the chicken drumsticks in the egg mixture.
8. Again coat the chicken drumsticks with the flour mixture.
9. Arrange the chicken drumsticks onto a wire rack-lined baking sheet and set aside for about 15 minutes.
10. Now, arrange the chicken drumsticks onto a sheet pan and spray the chicken with cooking spray lightly.
11. Press the "Power" button of the Ninja Foodi Digital Air Fry Oven and turn the dial to select "Air Fry" mode.
12. Press the "Time" button and again turn the dial to set the cooking time to 25 minutes.
13. Now push the "Temp" button and rotate the dial to set the temperature at 350°F.
14. Press the "Start/Pause" button to start.
15. When the unit beeps to show that it is preheated, open the lid and grease the air fry basket.
16. Place the chicken drumsticks into the prepared air fry basket and insert them in the Air Fry Oven.
17. When the cooking time is completed, open the lid and serve hot.

Serving Suggestions: Serve with French fries.

Variation Tip: Make sure to coat chicken pieces completely.

# Lemony Chicken Thighs

**Preparation time**
15 MINUTES

**Cooking time**
20 MINUTES

**Servings**
6

**Ratings**

## Ingredients

6 (6-oz.) chicken thighs

2 tbsp. olive oil

2 tbsp. fresh lemon juice

1 tbsp. Italian seasoning

Salt and ground black pepper, as required

1 lemon, sliced thinly

## Nutritional Info

Calories: 472

Fats: 18 g

Saturated Fats: 4.3 g

Carbs: 0.6 g

Fiber: 0.1 g

Sugar: 0.4 g

Protein: 49.3 g

## Directions

1. In a container, put all the fixings except for the lemon slices and toss to coat well.
2. Refrigerate to marinate for 30 minutes or overnight.
3. Remove the chicken thighs and let any excess marinade drip off.
4. Press the "Power" button of the Ninja Foodi Digital Air Fry Oven and turn the dial to select "Air Fry" mode.
5. Press the "Time" button and again turn the dial to set the cooking time to 20 minutes.
6. Now push the "Temp" button and rotate the dial to set the temperature at 350°F.
7. Press the "Start/Pause" button to start.
8. When the unit beeps to show that it is preheated, open the lid and grease the air fry basket.
9. Place the chicken thighs into the prepared air fry basket and insert them in the Air Fry Oven.
10. After 10 minutes of cooking, flip the chicken thighs.
11. When cooking time is completed, open the lid and serve hot alongside the lemon slices.

Serving Suggestions: Serve alongside your favorite dipping sauce.

Variation Tip: Select chicken with a pinkish hue.

# Chinese Chicken Drumsticks

 Preparation time
10 MINUTES

 Cooking time
20 MINUTES

Servings
4

## Ratings

★ ★ ★

## Ingredients

1 tbsp. oyster sauce

1 tsp. light soy sauce

½ tsp. sesame oil

1 tsp. Chinese five-spice powder

Salt and ground black pepper, as required

4 (6-oz.) chicken drumsticks

1 cup corn flour

## Nutritional Info

Calories: 287

Fats: 13.8 g

Saturated Fats: 7.1 g

Carbs: 1.6 g

Fiber: 0.2 g

Sugar: 0.1 g

Protein: 38.3 g

## Directions

1. In a bowl, mix together the sauces, oil, five-spice powder, salt, and black pepper.
2. Add the chicken drumsticks and coat them generously with the marinade.
3. Refrigerate for at least 30–40 minutes.
4. In a shallow dish, place the corn flour.
5. Remove the chicken from marinade and lightly coat with corn flour.
6. Press the "Power" button of the Ninja Foodi Digital Air Fry Oven and turn the dial to select "Air Fry" mode.
7. Press the "Time" button and again turn the dial to set the cooking time to 20 minutes.
8. Now push the "Temp" button and rotate the dial to set the temperature at 390°F.
9. Press the "Start/Pause" button to start.
10. When the unit beeps to show that it is preheated, open the lid and grease the air fry basket.
11. Place the chicken drumsticks into the prepared air fry basket and insert them in the Air Fry Oven.
12. When the cooking time is completed, open the lid and serve hot.

Serving Suggestions: Serve with fresh greens.

Variation Tip: Use best quality sauces.

# Crispy Chicken Thighs

**Preparation time**
15 MINUTES

**Cooking time**
25 MINUTES

**Servings**
4

Ratings

## Ingredients

½ cup all-purpose flour

1½ tbsp. Cajun seasoning

1 tsp. seasoning salt

1 egg

4 (4-oz.) chicken thighs, skin-on

## Nutritional Info

Calories: 288

Fats: 9.6 g

Saturated Fats: 2.7 g

Carbs: 12 g

Fiber: 0.4 g

Sugar: 0.1 g

Protein: 35.9 g

## Directions

1. In a container, add together the flour, Cajun seasoning, and seasoning salt.
2. In an extra bowl, crack the egg and beat well.
3. Coat each chicken thigh with the flour mixture, then dip them into the beaten egg and finally, coat them with the flour mixture again.
4. Shake off the excess flour thoroughly.
5. Press the "Power" button of the Ninja Foodi Digital Air Fry Oven and turn the dial to select "Air Fry" mode.
6. Press the "Time" and again turn the dial to set the cooking time to 25 minutes.
7. Now push the "Temp" and rotate the dial to set the temperature at 390°F.
8. Press the "Start/Pause" button to start.
9. When the unit beeps to show that it is preheated, open the lid and grease the air fry basket.
10. Place the chicken thighs into the prepared air fry basket and insert them in the Air Fry Oven.
11. When cooking time is completed, open the lid and serve hot.

Serving Suggestions: Serve with ketchup.

Variation Tip: Feel free to use seasoning of your choice.

# Oat Crusted Chicken Breasts

| Preparation time | Cooking time | Servings |
|---|---|---|
| 15 MINUTES | 12 MINUTES | 2 |

## Ratings

⭐ ⭐ ⭐

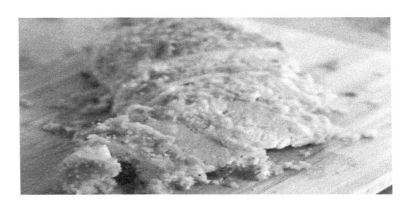

## Ingredients

2 (6-oz.) chicken breasts

Salt and ground black pepper, as required

¾ cup oats

2 tbsp. mustard powder

1 tbsp. fresh parsley

2 eggs

## Nutritional Info

Calories: 556

Fats: 22.2 g

Saturated Fats: 5.3 g

Carbs: 25.1 g

Fiber: 4.8 g

Sugar: 1.4 g

Protein: 61.6 g

## Directions

1. Put the chicken breasts onto a cutting board, and with a meat mallet, flatten each into an even thickness.
2. Then, cut each chicken breast in half.
3. Sprinkle the chicken pieces with salt and black pepper and set aside.
4. In a blender, add the oats, mustard powder, parsley, salt and black pepper and pulse until a coarse breadcrumb-like mixture is formed.
5. Transfer the oat mixture into a shallow bowl.
6. In another bowl, crack the eggs and beat well.
7. Coat the chicken with oat mixture, dip into beaten eggs, and coat with the oat mixture again.
8. Press the "Power" button of the Ninja Foodi Digital Air Fry Oven and turn the dial to select "Air Fry" mode.
9. Press the "Time" button and again turn the dial to set the cooking time to 12 minutes.
10. Now push the "Temp" and rotate the dial to set the temperature at 350°F.
11. Press the "Start/Pause" button to start.
12. When the unit beeps to show that it is preheated, open the lid and grease the air fry basket.
13. Place the chicken breasts into the prepared air fry basket and insert them in the Air Fry Oven.
14. Flip the chicken breasts once halfway through.
15. When cooking time is completed, open the lid and serve hot.

Serving Suggestions: Serve with mashed potatoes.

Variation Tip: Check the meat "best by" date.

# Crispy Chicken Cutlets

**Preparation time**
15 MINUTES

**Cooking time**
30 MINUTES

**Servings**
4

## Ratings

## Ingredients

¾ cup flour

2 large eggs

1½ cups breadcrumbs

¼ cup Parmesan cheese, grated

1 tbsp. mustard powder

Salt and ground black pepper, as required

4 (6-oz.) (¼-inch thick) skinless, boneless chicken cutlets

## Nutritional Info

Calories: 526

Fats: 13 g

Saturated Fats: 4.2 g

Carbs: 48.6 g

Fiber: 3 g

Sugar: 3 g

Protein: 51.7 g

## Directions

1. In a shallow bowl, add the flour.
2. In a another bowl, break the eggs and beat them well.
3. In a third bowl, mix together the breadcrumbs, cheese, mustard powder, salt, and black pepper.
4. Season the chicken with salt, and black pepper.
5. Coat the chicken with flour, then dip them into beaten eggs and finally coat them with the breadcrumbs mixture.
6. Press the "Power" button of the Ninja Foodi Digital Air Fry Oven and turn the dial to select "Air Fry" mode.
7. Press the "Time" button and again turn the dial to set the cooking time to 30 minutes.
8. Now push the "Temp" button and rotate the dial to set the temperature at 355°F.
9. Press the "Start/Pause" button to start.
10. When the unit beeps to show that it is preheated, open the lid and grease the air fry basket.
11. Place the chicken cutlets into the prepared air fry basket and insert them in the Air Fry Oven.
12. When the cooking time is completed, open the lid and serve hot.

Serving Suggestions: Serve with favorite greens.

Variation Tip: Parmesan cheese can be replaced with your favorite cheese.

# Brie Stuffed Chicken Breasts

| Preparation time | Cooking time | Servings |
|---|---|---|
| 15 MINUTES | 15 MINUTES | 4 |

### Ratings

## Ingredients

2 (8-oz.) skinless, boneless chicken fillets

Salt and ground black pepper, as required

4 brie cheese slices

1 tbsp. fresh chive, minced

4 bacon slices

## Nutritional Info

Calories: 394

Fats: 24 g

Saturated Fats: 10.4 g

Carbs: 0.6 g

Sugar: 0.1 g

Protein: 42 g

## Directions

1. Cut each chicken fillet in 2 equal-sized pieces.
2. Carefully, make a slit in each chicken piece horizontally, about ¼-inch from the edge.
3. Open each chicken piece and season them with salt and black pepper.
4. Place 1 cheese slice in the open area of each chicken piece and sprinkle with the chives.
5. Close the chicken pieces and wrap each one with a bacon slice.
6. Secure with toothpicks.
7. Press the "Power" button of th Ninja Foodi Digital Air Fry Oven and turn the dial to select "Air Fry" mode.
8. Press the "Time" button and again turn the dial to set the cooking time to 15 minutes.
9. Now push the "Temp" button and rotate the dial to set the temperature at 355°F.
10. Press the "Start/Pause" button to start.
11. When the unit beeps to show that it is preheated, open the lid and grease the air fry basket.
12. Place the chicken pieces into the prepared air fry basket and insert them in the oven.
13. When the cooking time is completed, open the lid and place the rolled chicken breasts onto a cutting board.
14. Cut into desired slice sizes and serve.

Serving Suggestions: Serve with creamy mashed potatoes.

Variation Tip: Season the chicken breasts slightly.

# Chicken Kabobs

 **Preparation time**
15 MINUTES

 **Cooking time**
9 MINUTES

 **Servings**
2

 **Ratings**

## Ingredients

1 (8-oz.) chicken breast, cut into -sized pieces

1 tbsp. fresh lemon juice

3 garlic cloves, grated

1 tbsp. fresh oregano, minced

½ tsp. lemon zest, grated

Salt and ground black pepper, as required

1 tsp. plain Greek yogurt

1 tsp. olive oil

## Nutritional Info

Calories: 167

Fats: 5.5 g

Saturated Fats: 0.5 g

Carbs: 3.4 g

Fiber: 0.5 g

Sugar: 1.1 g

Protein: 24.8 g

## Directions

1. In a container, add the chicken, lemon juice, garlic, oregano, lemon zest, salt and black pepper and toss to coat well.
2. Cover the bowl and refrigerate overnight.
3. Bring out the bowl from the refrigerator and stir in the yogurt and oil.
4. Thread the chicken pieces onto the metal skewers.
5. Press the "Power" button of the Ninja Foodi Digital Air Fry Oven and turn the dial to select "Air Fry" mode.
6. Press the "Time" button and again turn the dial to set the cooking time to 9 minutes.
7. Now push the "Temp" button and rotate the dial to set the temperature at 350°F.
8. Press "Start/Pause" button to start.
9. When the unit beeps to show that it is preheated, open the lid and grease the air fry basket.
10. Place the skewers into the prepared air fry basket and insert them in the oven.
11. Flip the skewers once halfway through.
12. When cooking time is completed, open the lid and serve hot.

Serving Suggestions: Serve alongside fresh salad.

Variation Tip: Make sure to tri the chicken pieces.

# Simple Turkey Breast

 Preparation time
10 MINUTES

 Cooking time
1 HOUR 20 MINUTES

Servings
6

 Ratings

## Ingredients

1 (2 ¾-lb.) turkey breast half, bone-in, skin-on

Salt and ground black pepper, as required

## Nutritional Info

Calories: 221

Fats: 0.8 g

Protein: 51.6 g

## Directions

1. Rub the turkey breast with the salt and black pepper evenly.
2. Arrange the turkey breast into a greased baking pan.
3. Press the "Power" button of the Ninja Foodi Digital Air Fry Oven and turn the dial to select "Air Bake" mode.
4. Press the "Time" and again turn the dial to set the cooking time to 1 hour 20 minutes.
5. Now push the "Temp" button and rotate the dial to set the temperature at 450°F.
6. Press the "Start/Pause" button to start.
7. Open the unit when it has reached the temperature, when it beeps.
8. Arrange the pan over the wire rack and insert it in the oven.
9. When cooking time is completed, open the lid and place the turkey breast onto a cutting board.
10. With a piece of foil, cover the turkey breast for about 20 minutes before slicing.
11. With a sharp knife, cut the turkey breast into desired size slices and serve.

Serving Suggestions: Serve alongside the steamed veggies.

Variation Tip: Beware of flat spots on meat, which can indicate thawing and refreezing.

# Herbed Duck Breast

**Preparation time**
15 MINUTES

**Cooking time**
20 MINUTES

**Servings**
2

## Ratings

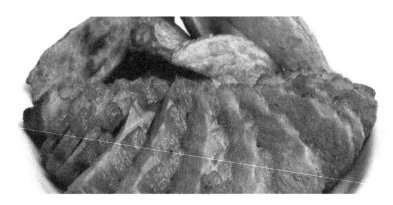

## Ingredients

1 (10-oz.) duck breast

Olive oil cooking spray

½ tbsp. fresh thyme, chopped

½ tbsp. fresh rosemary, chopped

1 cup chicken broth

1 tbsp. fresh lemon juice

Salt and ground black pepper, as required

## Nutritional Info

Calories: 209

Fats: 6.6 g

Saturated Fats: 0.3 g

Carbs: 1.6 g

Fiber: 0.6 g

Sugar: 0.5 g

Protein: 33.8 g

## Directions

1. Spray the duck breast with cooking spray evenly.
2. In a container, add the remaining ingredients.
3. Add the duck breast and coat it with the marinade generously.
4. Refrigerate it covered for about 4 hours.
5. With a piece of foil, cover the duck breast.
6. Press the "Power" of the Ninja Foodi Digital Air Fry Oven and turn the dial to select "Air Fry" mode.
7. Press the "Time" button and again turn the dial to set the cooking time to 15 minutes.
8. Now push the "Temp" and rotate the dial to set the temperature at 390°F.
9. Press the "Start/Pause" button to start.
10. When the unit beeps to show that it is preheated, open the lid and grease the air fry basket.
11. Place the duck breast into the prepared air fry basket and insert them in the Air Fry Oven.
12. After 15 minutes of cooking, set the temperature to 355°F for 5 minutes.
13. When the cooking time is completed, open the lid and serve hot.

Serving Suggestions: Serve with spiced potatoes.

Variation Tip: Don't undercook the duck meat.

Fish and Seafood

# Breaded Coconut Shrimp

**Preparation time**
5 MINUTES

**Cooking time**
15 MINUTES

**Servings**
4

## Ratings

## Ingredients

1 lb. shrimp
1 cup panko breadcrumbs
1 cup coconut, shredded
2 eggs
⅓ cup all-purpose flour

## Nutritional Info

Calories: 285
Fats: 12.8 g
Carbs: 3.7 g
Protein: 38.1 g

## Directions

1. Fix the temperature of the Air Fryer at 360° Fahrenheit.

2. Peel and devein the shrimp.

3. Whisk the seasonings with the flour as desired. In another bowl, whisk the eggs, and in the third bowl, combine the breadcrumbs and coconut.

4. Dip the cleaned shrimp into the flour, egg wash, and finish it off with the coconut mixture.

5. Lightly, spray the basket of the Air Fry Oven and set the timer for 10–15 minutes.

6. Air-fry until it's a golden brown before serving.

# Breaded Cod Sticks

 **Preparation time**
5 MINUTES

 **Cooking time**
20 MINUTES

**Servings**
4

## Ratings

## Ingredients

2 large eggs
3 tbsp. milk
2 cups breadcrumbs
1 cups almond flour
1 lb. cod

## Nutritional Info

Calories: 254
Fats: 14.2 g
Carbs: 5.7 g
Protein: 39.1 g

## Directions

1. Heat the Air Fry Oven to 350°F.

2. Prepare 3 bowls; one with the milk and eggs, one with the breadcrumbs (salt and pepper if desired), and another with almond flour.

3. Dip the sticks in the flour, egg mixture, and breadcrumbs.

4. Place in the basket and set the timer for 12 minutes. Toss the basket halfway through the cooking process.

5. Serve with your favorite sauce.

# Cajun Shrimp

**Preparation time**
5 MINUTES

**Cooking time**
5 MINUTES

**Servings**
6

**Ratings**

## Ingredients

16–20 (1 ¼-lb.) tiger shrimp
1 tbsp. olive oil
.5 tsp. OLD BAY® seasoning
.25 tsp. smoked paprika
.25 tsp. cayenne pepper

## Nutritional Info

Calories: 356
Fats: 18 g
Carbs: 5 g
Protein: 34 g

## Directions

1. Set the Air Fry Oven to 390° Fahrenheit.

2. Cover the shrimp using the oil and spices.

3. Toss them into the Air Fry basket and set the timer for 5 minutes.

4. Serve with your favorite side dish.

# Cod Fish Nuggets

**Preparation time**
5 MINUTES

**Cooking time**
20 MINUTES

**Servings**
4

## Ratings

### Ingredients

1 lb. cod fillet

3 eggs

4 tbsp. olive oil

1 cup almond flour

1 cup breadcrumbs, gluten-free

### Nutritional Info

Calories: 334

Fats: 10 g

Carbs: 8 g

Protein: 32 g

### Directions

1. Heat the Air Fry Oven to 390°F.

2. Slice the cod into nuggets.

3. Prepare 3 bowls and whisk the eggs in one of them. Combine the salt, oil, and breadcrumbs in another bowl. Sift the almond flour into the third bowl.

4. Cover each of the nuggets with the flour, dip in the eggs, and the breadcrumbs.

5. Arrange the nuggets in the basket and set the timer for 20 minutes.

6. Serve the fish with your favorite dips or sides.

# Creamy Salmon

**Preparation time**
5 MINUTES

**Cooking time**
20 MINUTES

**Servings**
4

Ratings

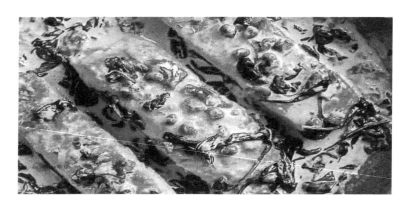

## Ingredients

1 tbsp. dill, chopped
1 tbsp. olive oil
1 ¾ oz. plain yogurt
6 pieces (¾-lb.) salmon

## Nutritional Info

Calories: 340
Carbs: 5 g
Fats: 16 g
Protein: 32 g

## Directions

1. Heat the Air Fry Oven and wait for it to reach 285°F.

2. Shake the salt over the salmon and add them to the fryer basket with the olive oil to air-fry for 10 minutes.

3. Whisk the yogurt, salt, and dill.

4. Serve the salmon with the sauce or side dish of your preference.

# Crumbled Fish

**Preparation time**
5 MINUTES

**Cooking time**
15 MINUTES

**Servings**
4

## Ratings

### Ingredients

.5 cup breadcrumbs

4 tbsp. vegetable oil

1 egg

4 fish fillets

1 lemon

### Nutritional Info

Calories: 320

Carbs: 8 g

Fats: 10 g

Protein: 28 g

### Directions

1. Heat the Air Fry Oven to 356°F.

2. Whisk the oil and breadcrumbs until crumbly.

3. Dip the fish into the egg, then in the crumb mixture.

4. Arrange the fish fillets in the Air Fry Oven and air-fry for 12 minutes.

5. Garnish with the lemon.

# Fried Catfish

**Preparation time**
5 MINUTES

**Cooking time**
15 MINUTES

**Servings**
4

## Ratings

### Ingredients

1 tbsp. olive oil
.25 cup seasoned fish fry
4 catfish fillets

### Nutritional Info

Calories: 376
Fats: 9 g
Carbs: 10 g
Protein: 28 g

### Directions

1. Heat the Air Fry Oven to 400°Fbefore 'fry' time.

2. Rinse the catfish and pat dry using a paper towel.

3. Dump the seasoning into a sizeable Ziploc® bag. Add the fish and shake to cover each fillet. Spray with the cooking oil spray and add to the basket.

4. Set the timer for 10 minutes. Flip, and reset the timer for ten additional minutes. Turn the fish once more and cook for 2–3 minutes.

5. Once it reaches the desired crispiness, transfer to a plate and serve.

# Grilled Sardines

**Preparation time**
5 MINUTES

**Cooking time**
20 MINUTES

**Servings**
4

**Ratings**

## Ingredients

5 sardines

## Nutritional Info

Calories: 189 g

Fats: 10 g

Protein: 22 g

Cholesterol: 128 mg

## Directions

1. Preheat the Air Fry Oven to 320°F.

2. Place the sardines in the air fry basket.

3. Set the timer to 14 minutes. After 7 minutes, remember to turn the sardines so that they are roasted on both sides.

# Zucchini with Tuna

 **Preparation time**
10 MINUTES

 **Cooking time**
30 MINUTES

 **Servings**
4

## Ratings

## Ingredients

4 zucchinis
4 1/5 oz. tuna in oil (canned) drained
1 oz. grated cheese
1 tsp. pine nuts
Salt, pepper to taste

## Nutritional Info

Calories: 389
Carbs: 10 g
Fats: 29 g
Sugar: 5 g
Protein: 23 g
Cholesterol: 40 mg

## Directions

1. Cut the zucchini in half, laterally, and empty it with a small spoon (set aside the pulp that will be used for filling); place them in the basket.

2. In a food processor, put the zucchini pulp, drained tuna, pine nuts and grated cheese. Mix everything until you get a homogeneous and dense mixture.

3. Fill the zucchini. Set the Air Fry Oven to 356°F.

4. Simmer for 20 min, depending on the size of the zucchini. Let cool before serving.

# Deep Fried Prawns

**Preparation time**
15 MINUTES

**Cooking time**
20 MINUTES

**Servings**
6

## Ratings

## Ingredients

12 prawns
2 eggs
½ tsp. Flour to taste
1 tbsp Breadcrumbs
4 tbsp Yogurt
2 tbsp Mayonnaise sauce

## Nutritional Info

Calories: 2385.1
Fats: 23
Carbs: 52.3 g
Sugar: 0.1 g
Protein: 21.4 g

## Directions

1. Remove the head of the prawns and shell carefully.

2. Dip the prawns first in the flour, then in the beaten eggs and then in the breadcrumbs.

3. Preheat the Air Fry Oven for 1 minute at 302°F.

4. Add the prawns and cook for 4 minutes. If the prawns are large, it will be necessary to cook 6 at a time.

5. Turn the prawns and cook for another 4 minutes.

6. They should be served with a yogurt or mayonnaise sauce.

# Mussels with Pepper

**Preparation time**
15 MINUTES

**Cooking time**
20 MINUTES

**Servings**
5

## Ratings

## Ingredients

1 ½ lb. mussels
1 clove garlic
1 tsp. oil
½ tsp. Pepper to taste
½ tsp. Parsley Taste

## Nutritional Info

Calories: 150
Carbs: 2 g
Fats: 8 g
Protein: 15 g

## Directions

1. Clean and scrape the mussels cover and remove the byssus (the "beard" that comes out of the mussels.)

2. Pour the oil, clean the mussels and the crushed garlic in the air fryer basket. Set the temperature to 392°F and simmer for 12 minutes. Towards the end of cooking, add the black pepper and the chopped parsley.

3. Finally, distribute the mussel juice well at the bottom of the basket, shaking the basket.

# Monkfish with Olives and Capers

 **Preparation time**
25 MINUTES

 **Cooking time**
40 MINUTES

**Servings**
4

## Ratings

## Ingredients

1 monkfish
10 cherry tomatoes
1 ¾ cailletier olives
5 capers

## Nutritional Info

Calories: 404
Fats: 29 g
Carbs: 36 g
Sugar: 7 g
Protein: 24 g
Cholesterol: 36 mg

## Directions

1. Spread aluminum foil inside the air fry basket and place the monkfish clean and skinless.

2. Chop the tomatoes and add them with the olives, capers, oil, and salt.

3. Set the temperature to 320°F.

4. Cook the monkfish for about 40 minutes.

# Shrimp Zucchini and Cherry Tomato Sauce

 **Preparation time**
5 MINUTES

 **Cooking time**
30 MINUTES

 **Servings**
4

## Ratings

## Ingredients

2 zucchinis
300 shrimps
7 cherry tomatoes
Salt and pepper to taste
1 garlic clove

## Nutritional Info

Calories: 214.3
Fats: 8.6 g
Carbs: 7.8 g
Sugar: 4.8 g
Protein: 27.0 g
Cholesterol: 232.7 mg

## Directions

1. Pour the oil in the Air Fry Oven, and add the garlic clove and diced zucchini.

2. Cook for 15 minutes at 302°F.

3. Add the shrimps and the tomato pieces, salt, and spices.

4. Cook for another 5−10 minutes or until the shrimp water evaporates.

# Salmon with Pistachio Bark

**Preparation time**
10 MINUTES

**Cooking time**
30 MINUTES

**Servings**
4

## Ratings

### Ingredients

1 ⅓ lb. salmon fillet

1 ⅓ oz. pistachios

Salt to taste

### Nutritional Info

Calories: 371.7

Fats: 21.8 g

Carbs: 9.4 g

Sugar: 2.2 g

Protein: 34.7 g

Cholesterol: 80.5 mg

### Directions

1. Put the parchment paper on the bottom of the air fryer basket and place the salmon fillet in it (it can be cooked whole or already divided into four portions).

2. Cut the pistachios in thick pieces, grease the top of the fish, and salt (little because the pistachios are already salted), and cover everything with the pistachios.

3. Set the air fryer to 356°F and simmer for 25 minutes.

# Salted Marinated Salmon

**Preparation time**
10 MINUTES

**Cooking time**
30 MINUTES

**Servings**
4

## Ratings

## Ingredients

1 lb. salmon fillet

16 lb. coarse salt

1 tbsp Oil

## Nutritional Info

Calories: 290

Fats: 13 g

Carbs: 3 g

Protein: 40 g

Cholesterol: 196 mg

## Directions

1. Place some baking paper on the air fry basket and the salmon on top (skin-side up) covered with coarse salt.

2. Set the air fryer to 302°F.

3. Cook everything for 25–30 minutes. At the end of cooking, remove the fish and serve with a drizzle of oil.

# Sautéed Trout with Almonds

**Preparation time**
35 MINUTES

**Cooking time**
20 MINUTES

**Servings**
4

## Ratings

## Ingredients

1 1/5 lb. salmon trout
15 black peppercorns
2 Dill leaves to taste
1 oz. almonds
½ tsp. Salt to taste
1 tbsp Oil

## Directions

1. Cut the trout into cubes and marinate it for half an hour with the rest of the ingredients (except salt).

2. Cook in air fryer for 17 minutes at 320°F. Drizzle with oil and salt and serve.

## Nutritional Info

Calories: 238.5
Fats: 20.1 g
Carbs: 11.5 g
Sugar: 1.0 g
Protein: 4.0 g
Cholesterol: 45.9 mg

# Calamari Slices

 **Preparation time**
5 MINUTES

 **Cooking time**
12 MINUTES

 **Servings**
4

## Ratings

## Ingredients

16 calamari slices
1 egg
1 tbsp Breadcrumbs
½ tsp. Salt, pepper, sweet paprika

## Nutritional Info

Calories: 356
Fats: 18 g
Carbs: 5 g
Protein: 34 g

## Directions

1. Put the calamari slices in the air fryer to boil for 2 minutes.

2. Remove and dry them well.

3. Beat the egg and season to taste. Add the egg mixture to the calamari slices and serve with the breadcrumbs.

# Honey Glazed Salmon

| Preparation time | Cooking time | Servings |
|---|---|---|
| 10 MINUTES | 8 MINUTES | 2 |

## Ratings

## Ingredients

2 (6-oz.) salmon fillets

½ tsp. Salt, as required

2 tbsp. honey

## Nutritional Info

Calories: 289

Fats: 10.5 g

Carbs: 17.3 g

Protein: 33.1 g

## Directions

1. Sprinkle the salmon fillets with salt and then, coat with honey.

2. Press the "Power" button of the Air Fry Oven and turn the dial to select the "Air Fry" mode.

3. Press the "Time" button and again turn the dial to set the cooking time to 8 minutes.

4. Now push the "Temp" button and rotate the dial to set the temperature at 355°F.

5. Press the "Start/Pause" button to start.

6. Open the unit when it is already hot, when it beeps.

7. Arrange the salmon fillets in a greased air fry basket and insert them in the Air Fry Oven.

8. Serve hot.

# Sweet and Sour Glazed Salmon

**Preparation time**
12 MINUTES

**Cooking time**
20 MINUTES

**Servings**
2

## Ratings

## Ingredients

⅓ cup soy sauce

⅓ cup honey

3 tsp. rice wine vinegar

1 tsp. water

4 (3 ½-oz.) salmon fillets

## Nutritional Info

Calories: 462

Fats: 12.3 g

Carbs: 49.8 g

Protein: 41.3 g

## Directions

1. Mix the soy sauce, honey, vinegar, and water together in a bowl.
2. In another small bowl, reserve about half of the mixture.
3. Add the salmon fillets in the remaining mixture and coat them well.
4. Cover the bowl and refrigerate to marinate for about 2 hours.
5. Press the "Power" button of the Air Fry Oven and turn the dial to select the "Air Fry" mode.
6. Press the "Time" button and again turn the dial to set the cooking time to 12 minutes.
7. Now push the "Temp" button and rotate the dial to set the temperature at 355°F.
8. Press the "Start/Pause" button to start.
9. Open the unit when it is already hot, when it beeps.
10. Arrange the salmon fillets in greased air fry basket" and insert them in the Air Fry Oven.
11. Flip the salmon fillets once halfway through and coat them with the reserved marinade after every 3 minutes.
12. Serve hot.

# Ranch Tilapia

**Preparation time**
15 MINUTES

**Cooking time**
13 MINUTES

**Servings**
4

## Ratings

## Ingredients

¾ cup cornflakes, crushed

1 (1-oz.) packet dry ranch-style dressing mix

2 ½ tbsp. vegetable oil

2 eggs

4 (6-oz.) tilapia fillets

## Nutritional Info

Calories: 267

Fats: 12.2 g

Carbs: 5.1 g

Protein: 34.9 g

## Directions

1. In a shallow bowl, beat the eggs.

2. In another bowl, add the cornflakes, ranch dressing, and oil and mix until a crumbly mixture form.

3. Dip the tilapia fillets into the egg mixture and then, and coat them with the bread crumbs mixture.

4. Press the "Power" button of the Air Fry Oven and turn the dial to select the "Air Fry" mode.

5. Press the "Time" button and again turn the dial to set the cooking time to 13 minutes.

6. Now push the "Temp" button and rotate the dial to set the temperature at 356°F.

7. Press the "Start/Pause" button to start.

8. Open the unit when it is already hot, when it beeps.

9. Arrange the tilapia fillets in greased air fry basket and insert them in the Air Fry Oven.

10. Serve hot.

# Simple Haddock

**Preparation time**
15 MINUTES

**Cooking time**
8 MINUTES

**Servings**
2

## Ratings

## Ingredients

2 (6-oz.) haddock fillets

1 tbsp. olive oil

Salt and ground black pepper, as required

## Nutritional Info

Calories: 251

Fats: 8.6 g

Saturated Fats: 1.3 g

Cholesterol: 126 mg

Sodium 226: mg

Protein: 41.2 g

## Directions

1. Coat the haddock fillets with oil and then sprinkle with salt and black pepper.

2. Press the "Power" button of the Air Fry Oven and turn the dial to select the "Air Fry" mode.

3. Press the "Time" button and again turn the dial to set the cooking time to 8 minutes.

4. Now push the "Temp" button and rotate the dial to set the temperature at 355°F.

5. Press the "Start/Pause" button to start.

6. Open the unit when it is already hot, when it beeps.

7. Arrange the haddock fillets in a greased air fry basket and insert them in the Air Fry Oven.

8. Serve hot.

# Sesame Seeds Coated Tuna

 **Preparation time**
15 MINUTES

 **Cooking time**
6 MINUTES

**Servings**
2

 **Ratings**

## Ingredients

1 egg white

¼ cup white sesame seeds

1 tbsp. black sesame seeds

Salt and ground black pepper, as required

2 (6-oz.) tuna steaks

## Nutritional Info

Calories: 450

Total Fats: 21.9 g

Saturated Fats: 4.3 g

Cholesterol: 83 mg

Sodium: 182 mg

Carbs: 5.4 g

Fiber: 2.7 g

Sugar: 0.2 g

Protein: 56.7 g

## Directions

1. Mix the egg white in a container.

2. In another bowl, mix together the sesame seeds, salt, and black pepper.

3. Dip the tuna steaks into the beaten egg white and then coat with the sesame seeds mixture.

4. Press the "Power" button of the Air Fry Oven and turn the dial to select the "Air Fry" mode.

5. Press the "Time" button and again turn the dial to set the cooking time to 6 minutes.

6. Now push the "Temp" button and rotate the dial to set the temperature at 400 degrees F.

7. Press the "Start/Pause" button to start.

8. Open the unit when it is already hot, when it beeps.

9. Arrange the tuna steaks in greased "Air Fry Basket" and insert them in the Air Fry Oven.

10. Flip the tuna steaks once halfway through.

11. Serve hot.

# Air Fried Seafood

**Preparation time**
10 MINUTES

**Cooking time**
10 MINUTES

**Servings**
4

## Ratings

### Ingredients

1 lb. fresh scallops, mussels, fish fillets, prawns, shrimp

2 eggs, lightly beaten

Salt and black pepper

1 cup breadcrumbs mixed with the zest of 1 lemon

Cooking spray

### Nutritional Info

Calories: 133
Protein: 17.4 g
Fats: 3.1 g
Carbs: 8.2 g

### Directions

1. Clean the seafood as needed.

2. Dip the piece into the egg mixture and season with salt and pepper.

3. Coat the seafood in the crumbs and spray with oil.

4. Arrange the seafood in the Air Fry Oven and cook for 6 minutes at 400°F. turning once halfway through.

5. Serve and Enjoy!

Pork Beef
and Lamb

# Mexican Pork Stir Fry

 **Preparation time**
15 MINUTES

 **Cooking time**
15 MINUTES

 **Servings**
4

## Ratings

## Ingredients

12 oz. pork tenderloin
4 slices hickory bacon, chopped
1 chipotle chili, chopped
1 tbsp. olive oil
1 tsp. cumin
1 tsp. oregano
2 cloves garlic, chopped
1 red bell pepper, cut into strips
1 onion, halved and sliced thin
3 cups lettuce, chopped

## Nutritional Info

Calories: 322 calories
Total Carbohydrate: 5 g
Total Fat: 4g
Protein: 34 g
Sodium: 192 mg

## Directions

1. Slice tenderloin in half lengthwise, and then cut crosswise thinly. Toss pork, bacon, and chipotle pieces together in a small bowl; set aside.

2. Add oil, cumin, oregano, and garlic to the cooking pot. Set to sauté on med-high heat.

3. Include bell pepper and onion and cook, stirring frequently, 3-4 minutes until tender-crisp. Transfer to a bowl.

4. Add pork mixture to the pot and cook, frequently stirring, 3-4 minutes until bacon is crisp and pork is no longer pink.

5. Return vegetables to the pot and cook until heated through. Serve over a bed of lettuce.

# Simple Beef and Shallot Curry

 **Preparation time**
1 HOUR

 **Cooking time**
40 MINUTES

**Servings**
4

## Ratings

## Ingredients

1 lb. beef stew meat

1/4 tsp. salt

1/8 tsp. turmeric

2 tbsp. olive oil

2 tbsp. shallots, sliced

1 tbsp. fresh ginger, grated

1 tbsp. garlic, chopped fine

3 cups of water

2 tsp. fish sauce

8 shallots, peeled and left whole

1/2 tsp. chili powder

## Nutritional Info

Calories: 322 calories

Total Carbohydrate: 5 g

Total Fat: 4g

Protein: 34 g

## Directions

1. Mix the beef, salt, and turmeric, use your fingers to massage the seasonings into the meat. Cover and refrigerate for 1 hour.

2. Add the oil to the cooking pot and set to sauté on med-high.

3. Add the sliced shallot and cook until golden brown, 6-8 minutes. Transfer to a bowl.

4. Include the garlic and ginger to the pot and cook for 1 minute or until fragrant.

5. Put the beef and cook until no pink shows, about 5-6 minutes. Stir in the water and fish sauce until combined.

6. Add the lid and set to pressure cook on high. Set the timer for 20 minutes. When the timer goes off, use the manual release to remove the pressure.

7. Set back to sauté on med-high and add the fried shallots, whole shallots, and chili powder. Cook, frequently stirring, until shallots are soft and the sauce has thickened about 10 minutes. Serve.

# Polynesian Pork Burger

 **Preparation time**
15 MINUTES

 **Cooking time**
20 MINUTES

**Servings**
4

## Ratings

## Ingredients

1 lb. ground pork

1/4 cup green onion, chopped fine

1/8 tsp. allspice

1/8 tsp. salt

1/8 tsp. pepper

1/2 tsp. ginger

4 pineapple rings

1/4 cup barbecue sauce

4 burger buns

4 large lettuce leaves

1/4 lb. ham, sliced thin

## Nutritional Info

Calories: 155 calories

Total Carbohydrate: 13 g

Total Fat: 12g

Protein: 10

Sodium 5g

## Directions

1.  Spray the rack and place it in the cooking pot.

2.  In a large bowl, combine pork, green onion, allspice, salt, pepper, and ginger until thoroughly mixed. Form into 4 patties.

3.  Put the patties on the rack and brush the tops with barbecue sauce. Cook patties 5-7 minutes, flip and brush with barbecue sauce, cook another 5-7 minutes. Place the patties on the bottom of the cooking pot.

4.  Spray the rack with cooking spray again. Lay the pineapple rings on the rack. Cook 3-5 minutes per side. Transfer pineapple and patties to a serving plate and let sit 5 minutes.

5.  Place the buns on the rack, cut side up, and toast. To serve; top-bottom bun with lettuce, patty barbecue sauce, ham, pineapple, and top bun. Repeat. Serve immediately.

# Ham Ricotta and Zucchini Fritters

 **Preparation time**
10 MINUTES

 **Cooking time**
10 MINUTES

**Servings**
4

## Ratings

## Ingredients

1 1/2 tbsp. butter, unsalted
1/3 cup milk
1/2 cup ricotta cheese
2 eggs
1 1/2 tsp. Baking powder
1/2 tsp. Salt
1/4 tsp. pepper
1 cup flour
1/4 cup fresh basil, chopped
3 oz. ham, cut in strips
1/2 zucchini, cut into
matchsticks

## Nutritional Info

Calories: 180 calories
Total Carbohydrate: 15 g
Total Fat: 15
Protein: 7
Sodium 451 g
Potassium: 176 mg

## Directions

1. Spray the fryer sheet with cooking spray. Place in the cooking pot.

2. Take the butter in a microwave-safe bowl until melted.

3. Whisk milk and ricotta into melted butter until smooth. Whisk in eggs until combined.

4. Stir in baking powder, salt, and pepper until combined. Stir in flour until combined.

5. Fold in basil, ham, and zucchini until distributed evenly. Drop batter by ¼ cups into a fryer basket, and these will need to be cooked in batches.

6. Add the tender-crisp lid and set it to air fry at 375°F. Cook fritters 4-5 minutes per side until golden brown and cooked through. Serve immediately.

# Healthier Meatloaf

**Preparation time**
10 MINUTES

**Cooking time**
10 MINUTES

**Servings**
4

## Ratings

★ ★ ★

## Ingredients

Nonstick cooking spray
1 lb. lean ground pork
1 cup oats
8 oz. tomato sauce, divided
1 onion, chopped fine
1/2 cup zucchini, grated and excess liquid squeezed out
1 clove garlic, chopped fine
1 egg, lightly beaten
1 tsp. salt
1/8 tsp. pepper
½ tsp. Italian seasoning

## Nutritional Info

Calories: 355 calories
Total Carbohydrate: 36 g
Total Fat: 30g
Protein: 33 g
Sodium 947 mg
Potassium: 810 mg

## Directions

1. Spray the cooking pot with cooking spray.

2. In a large bowl, combine pork, oats, half the tomato sauce, onion, zucchini, garlic, egg, salt, pepper, and Italian seasoning, and mix well.

3. Fold a big sheet of foil in half, then in half again. Place along the bottom up two sides of the cooking pot.

4. Add the pork mixture and form into a loaf shape. Spoon remaining tomato sauce over the top.

5. Add the lid and set it to slow cook on low. Cook 6 hours or until meatloaf is cooked through.

# Bacon Wrapped Hot Dogs

**Preparation time**
15 MINUTES

**Cooking time**
15 MINUTES

**Servings**
8

**Ratings**

## Ingredients

4 beef hot dogs

4 bacon strips

Cooking spray

4 bakery hot dog buns, split and toasted

1/2 red onion, chopped

1 cup sauerkraut, rinsed and drained

## Nutritional Info

Calories: 336 calories

Total Carbohydrate: 27 g

Total Fat: 17 g

Protein: 20 g

Sodium 129 mg

## Directions

1. Place Cook and Crisp Basket in the pot. Close crisping lid. Select AIR CRISP, set temperature to 360°F, and set time to 5 minutes. Select START/STOP to begin preheating.

2. Wrap each hot dog with bacon, securing it with toothpicks as needed.

3. Once the unit has preheated, open the lid and coat the basket with cooking spray. Place the hot dogs in the basket in a single layer. Close crisping lid.

4. Select AIR CRISP, set the temperature to 360°F, and set the time to 15 minutes. Select START/STOP to begin.

5. After 20 minutes, check doneness. If needed, continue cooking until it reaches your desired doneness.

6. When cooking is complete, place the hot dog in the buns with the onion and sauerkraut. Top, if desired, with condiments of your choice, such as yellow mustard, ketchup, or mayonnaise.

# Southern Style Lettuce Wraps

 **Preparation time**
10 MINUTES

 **Cooking time**
30 MINUTES

 **Servings**
8

## Ratings

## Ingredients

3 pounds boneless pork shoulder, cut into 1- to 2-inch cubes

2 cups light beer

1 cup brown sugar

1 teaspoon chipotle chills in adobo sauce

1 cup barbecue sauce

1 head iceberg lettuce, quartered and leaves separated

1 cup roasted peanuts, chopped or ground

Cilantro leaves

## Nutritional Info

Calories: 811 calories

Total Carbohydrate: 27 g

Total Fat: 18 g

Protein: 22 g

Sodium 130 mg

## Directions

1. Place the pork, beer, brown sugar, chipotle, and barbecue sauce in the pot.

2. Select PRESSURE and set to HI. Set the timer to 30 minutes. Select START/STOP to begin.

3. When pressure cooking is processed, release the pressure. Gently remove the lid when the unit has finished releasing pressure.

4. Using a silicone-tipped utensil a shred the pork in the pot. Mix the meat in with the sauce.

5. Place a small amount of pork in a piece of lettuce. Top with peanuts and cilantro to serve.

# Cheesy Taco Pasta Bake

 **Preparation time**
10 MINUTES

 **Cooking time**
20 MINUTES

**Servings**
6

 **Ratings**

★ ★ ★

## Ingredients

1 tablespoon extra-virgin olive oil
1 small onion, diced
1 pound ground beef
1 packet taco seasoning
1 (14.5-ounce) can chop tomatoes
1 (4-ounce) can diced green chills
1 (16-ounce) box dry elbow pasta
4 cups beef broth
2 ounces cream cheese, cut into pieces
3 cups shredded Mexican blend cheese, divided
Optional toppings:
Sour cream, for garnish
Red onion, for garnish
Chopped cilantro, for garnish

## Nutritional Info

Calories: 811 calories
Total Carbohydrate: 27 g
Total Fat: 18 g
Protein: 22 g
Sodium 130 mg

## Directions

1. Choose SEAR/SAUTÉ and set to medium. Select START to begin. Let preheat for 5 minutes.

2. Place the oil, onion, and beef in the pot and cook for about 5 minutes Add the taco seasoning and mix until the beef is coated.

3. Add the tomatoes, green chills, pasta, and beef broth.

4. Select PRESSURE and set to LO. Set time to 0 minutes. Select START/STOP to begin.

5. When pressure cooking is processed, allow the heat to naturally release for 10 minutes. After 10 minutes, let go the remaining pressure.

6. Mix together the cream cheese and the cheese. Stir well to melt cheese, and ensure all ingredients are combined.

7. Select BROIL. Select START/STOP to begin.

8. When cooking is complete, serve immediately.

# Fresh Kielbasa and Braised Sweet and Sour Cabbage

**Preparation time**
10 MINUTES

**Cooking time**
1 HOUR

**Servings**
6

## Ratings

## Ingredients

11/2 pounds fresh kielbasa sausage links

1/2 stick (¼ cup) unsalted butter

1/2 medium onion, thinly sliced

2 garlic cloves, minced

1 large head red cabbage, cut into ¼-inch slices

1/4 cup granulated sugar

1/3 cup apple cider vinegar

1/2 cup water

2 teaspoons caraway seeds

Kosher salt

Freshly ground black pepper

## Nutritional Info

Calories: 351 calories

Total Carbohydrate: 24 g

Total Fat: 19 g

Protein: 30 g

Sodium 200 mg

## Directions

1. Insert Cook and Crisp Basket into pot and close crisping lid. Select **AIR CRISP**, set temperature to 390°F, and set time to 15 minutes. Select START/STOP to begin. Let preheat for 5 minutes.

2. Add the sausage to the basket. Close lid and cook for 10 minutes.

3. When cooking is complete, open the lid and remove the basket and sausage. Set aside.

4. Select **SEAR/SAUTÉ** and set to HI. Select START/STOP to begin.

5. Add the butter and let it heat for 5 minutes. Add the onion and garlic and cook for 3 minutes.

6. Add the cabbage, sugar, vinegar, water, and caraway seeds, and season with salt and pepper.

7. Select **PRESSURE** and set to HI. Set time to 10 minutes. Select START/STOP to begin.

8. When pressure cooking is complete, quick release of the pressure by moving the pressure release valve to the VENT position.

9. Select **SEAR/SAUTÉ** and set to HI. Set time to 10 minutes. Select START/STOP to begin.

10. After 10 minutes, open the device and add the sausage to the top of the cabbage. Close the lid and continue cooking.

11. When cooking is complete, open the lid and serve.

# French Dip Sandwich

 **Preparation time**
10 MINUTES

 **Cooking time**
1 HOUR

**Servings**
6

 **Ratings**

## Ingredients

2 pounds beef rump roast, cut into large chunks
1 teaspoon paprika
1 teaspoon dried mustard
1 teaspoon garlic powder
1 teaspoon onion powder
1/2 teaspoon of sea salt
1/4 teaspoon freshly ground black pepper
2 cups beef stock
1 tablespoon Worcestershire sauce
1 teaspoon balsamic vinegar
1 loaf French bread, cut into 4 even pieces, then sliced in half
8 slices provolone cheese

## Nutritional Info

Calories: 351 calories
Total Carbohydrate: 24 g
Total Fat: 19 g
Protein: 30 g
Sodium 200 mg

## Directions

1. Place the meat in the bottom of the pot.
2. In a small mixing bowl, stir together the paprika, dried mustard, garlic powder, onion powder, salt, and pepper. Sprinkle this over the chunks of meat in the pot.
3. Add the beef stock, Worcestershire sauce, and balsamic vinegar. Fix the Pressure Lid, making sure the pressure release valve is in the Seal position.
4. When pressure cooking is processed, release the pressure by moving the pressure release valve to the Vent position. Gently remove the lid when the pressure has finished releasing.
5. Remove the meat from the pot and use two forks to shred it.
6. Carefully strain the juice from the pot. This is best done by lining a fine-mesh sieve with cheesecloth. Discard the solids and reserve the juice for dipping.
7. Place the meat back in the bottom of the pot.
8. Arrange the bread on the rack open-side up, and top each piece of bread with 1 slice of provolone cheese.
9. Remove the bread from the rack. Carefully remove the rack from the pot and use tongs to layer the meat on half of the cheesy bread slices. Top with the remaining cheesy bread slices and serve.

# Beef Empanadas

 **Preparation time**
15 MINUTES

 **Cooking time**
23 MINUTES

 **Servings**
2

## Ratings

## Ingredients

1 tablespoon extra-virgin olive oil
1/2 small white onion, finely chopped
1/4 pound 80% lean ground beef
1 garlic clove, minced
6 green olives, pitted and chopped
1/4 teaspoon paprika
1/4 teaspoon ground cumin
1/8 teaspoon ground cinnamon
2 small tomatoes, chopped
8 square gloze wrappers
1 egg, beaten

## Nutritional Info

Calories: 394 calories
Total Carbohydrate: 30 g
Total Fat: 25 g
Protein: 15 g
Sodium 250 mg

## Directions

1. Choose Sauté and set it to Medium-High. Select Start/Stop to begin. Let the pot to preheat for 8 minutes.

2. Put the oil, onion, ground beef, and garlic in the preheated pot and cook for 5 minutes, stirring occasionally.

3. Stir in the olives, paprika, cumin, and cinnamon and cook for an additional 3 minutes, and add the tomatoes.

4. Carefully remove the beef mixture from the pot.

5. Place the Cook and Crisp Basket in the pot. Close the Crisping Lid. Preheat the unit by selecting Air Crisp, setting the temperature to 400°F and setting the time to 5 minutes.

6. While the Ninja® Foodi™ is preheating, arrange the gloze wrappers on a flat surface. Place 1 to 2 tablespoons of the beef mixture in the center of each wrapper.

7. Redo steps 7 and 8 with the remaining empanadas.

# Pork Teriyaki with Rice

 **Preparation time**
15 MINUTES

 **Cooking time**
2 MINUTES

**Servings**
4

## Ratings

★ ★ ★

## Ingredients

1 cup long-grain white rice

1 cup water

1 head broccoli, trimmed into florets

1 tablespoon extra-virgin olive oil

1/4 teaspoon of sea salt

1/4 teaspoon freshly ground black pepper

1 pork tenderloin,

1 cup teriyaki sauce

Nonstick cooking spray

Sesame seeds, for garnish

## Nutritional Info

Calories: 400 calories

Total Carbohydrate: 25 g

Total Fat: 1109 g

Protein: 15 g

Sodium 200 mg

## Directions

1. Add the rice and water in the pot and stir to combine. Fix the Pressure Lid, making sure the pressure release valve is in the Seal position. Select Pressure and set to High. Set the time to 2 minutes, and then choose Start/Stop to begin.

2. Meanwhile, in a large mixing bowl, toss the broccoli with the olive oil. Season with salt and black pepper. In a medium mixing bowl, toss the pork with the teriyaki sauce until well coated.

3. When pressure cooking of the rice is processed, release the pressure by moving the pressure release valve to the Vent position. Gently remove the lid when the pressure has finished releasing.

4. . Spray the rack with cooking spray. Place the pork pieces on the rack. Arrange the broccoli around the pork.

5. Close the Crisping Lid. Select Broil and set the time to 12 minutes. Press Start/Stop to begin.

6. After cooking is complete, check for your desired crispiness and remove the rack from the pot. Serve the pork and broccoli over the rice, garnished with sesame seeds.

# Lamb Fingers

**Preparation time**
20 MINUTES

**Cooking time**
10 MINUTES

**Servings**
2

## Ratings

## Ingredients

1/2 cup crushed cornflakes

1 tablespoon fresh coriander, stems removed and chopped

1/4 teaspoon garlic minced

Sea salt and pepper (to taste)

1/4 cup coconut flour

1 eggs whisked

8 mini lamb fillers

## Nutritional Info

Calories: 294 calories

Total Carbohydrate: 20 g

Total Fat: 200 g

Protein: 21 g

Sodium 110 mg

## Directions

1. Cover each lamb fillet in coconut flour, then dip in the egg mixture and coat in cornflakes crushed. Follow until all of the lamb fillets are coated

2. Place the cook and crisp basket into the Foodi, close the lid and press the BAKE/ROAST setting at 200°C. Set for 5 minutes to preheat. Spray fillets with oil and place half in the basket. Set timer to 10 minutes. Cook in batches until done(75°C) and flip halfway through

3. Spray fillets with oil and place half of them in the basket. Set the timer to 10 minutes. Cook in batches until done, flipping halfway through.

Conclusions

By now you should have all the information regarding this incredible air furnace and its endless possibilities. In any case, we've tried to direct our efforts towards the well-being of you and your family, taking into account what your priorities, tastes and lifestyle are, and, in the end, we think we've done a good job if you start enjoying the benefits of this all-in-one appliance that will bring you smart-style cooking. This simple guide is your key to getting the most out of your multicooker, so take your time as you try out our recipes and remember to enjoy the experience of these Air Fry oven cooking wonders!

Thank you and enjoy your tasting!

CPSIA information can be obtained
at www.ICGtesting.com
Printed in the USA
LVHW062320180721
693060LV00002B/158